ROUGH POINT

THE NEWPORT HOME OF DORIS DUKE

Written by
A. Bruce MacLeish and Pieter N. Roos

Foreword

For over a century Rough Point has kept its secrets. Secluded behind a granite wall on one side and imposing cliffs on the other, the house has remained a mystery to local citizens and visitors to Newport alike, but the gates were never open until 2000. Doris Duke's bequest of her house as a museum means the public can now see the remarkable legacy of the Duke family in the magnificent site that Frederick Vanderbilt first envisioned in 1888.

Rough Point stands out amongst historic houses. Its location on the ocean is simultaneously dramatic and refined, a spectacular setting in a city that is renowned for its vistas. But what lies outside is surpassed by what lies within. The collection accumulated by the Dukes sits undisturbed and exactly as it was when Doris Duke last left the house in 1992. Few houses can make that claim, and fewer yet can claim such distinguished collections. Canvases by Gainsborough, van Dyck, and Renoir populate the house, at home among furniture and other decorative arts of equal caliber.

Miss Duke's legacy is remarkable. During her life she restored a sizable portion of 18th-century Newport by founding the Newport Restoration Foundation in the 1960s. At her death, not only did she leave Rough Point, but also two other of her residences, Duke Farms in Somerville, New Jersey, and Shangri La in Honolulu, to public, educational uses. The Doris Duke Charitable Foundation, created by her will, continues to do enormous good by funding vital public needs.

The Newport Restoration Foundation is pleased to invite you, through these pages, to tour one of America's finest historic houses and enjoy the charms of Rough Point, as did the families who lived here.

Pieter N. Roos
EXECUTIVE DIRECTOR
NEWPORT RESTORATION FOUNDATION

Contents

This postcard view of Rough Point of about 1908 shows the house with large porches facing the sea and ivy growing on the walls. Note that Frederick Vanderbilt's arched stone Cliff Walk bridge was still standing.

Rough Point's Architecture

Frederick Vanderbilt

In 1887, Frederick Vanderbilt commissioned the largest house that the Newport summer colony had yet seen. It was the latest local monument to Gilded Age wealth, constructed solidly in granite and sandstone and placed in a beautiful and dramatic setting. For an appropriate name, Vanderbilt took an old moniker for the obscure, water-washed promontory that borders the property. For just over a century, Rough Point served as the home of three families whose taste never wavered from the romantic vision of a summer home that married the sea, the rugged coastline, and the house.

Frederick and Louise Vanderbilt vacationed in Newport for some years in rented properties before they committed to buying land and building their own house. It started with the purchase in 1887 of a wood frame house and land belonging to William W. Tucker, but what Frederick acquired was only the first half of the property we know today. It was not until the following year that he managed to acquire an adjacent second home and lot belonging to Jacob Dunnell and to combine the two parcels to form one of the finest properties in southern Newport. It is a corner plot of nearly ten acres that overlooks Ochre Point and Middletown in one direction, and the Atlantic in the other, and frames them both with the rugged beauty of the rocky coastline. Frederick, a younger brother of the various Vanderbilts who undertook the building boom that transformed Newport by producing both the Breakers and Marble House, was the first in the family to undertake a new house. The design was more conservative than his older brothers' grand palaces, and today recalls a period of local summer housing that, although large in scale, was less ostentatious than what followed.

Vanderbilt's choice of the architectural firm of Peabody & Stearns has had the most lasting effect since every subsequent architect's alterations to the house closely followed the style of the original design. The firm, well-known in its own time, is still recognized for its contributions to New England's architecture at the turn of the 20th century. Locally, they designed a number of houses for Newport's summer colonists, among them Vinland and the original Breakers, which belonged to Frederick's sister and brother respectively.

Rough Point was designed in what has best been described as the English manorial style, the intent being to evoke the feel of an English country house. In reality, Peabody & Stearns's design is an

This photograph is one of the only known views of Rough Point's front façade during the Vanderbilt era. Because of the seamless nature of the later additions, at first glance it may not appear to have changed much in the last hundred years, but more careful examination soon reveals how much shorter the house was originally, and that the main stair is substantially different. One of the minor architectural mysteries of the house is the question of its portico. Most houses of this size and style proudly displayed this bit of architectural formality, and Rough Point's entrance seems ripe for one, but there is no evidence that a portico was ever designed, and it was certainly never built.

interpretation of different English styles of the 16th and 17th centuries; the result is not English at all but unmistakably American. Where the original English country house is a form that usually was added to haphazardly over the centuries, Rough Point is a well-organized and carefully conceived design—modern for its day and replete with the latest services and efficiencies of the 1890s.

The Vanderbilts' tenure at Rough Point was followed by the brief ownership of William and Nancy Leeds, who purchased the house when it was only seventeen years old. Perhaps because it was relatively new, they made no substantial changes. Although they hired John Russell Pope to make some alterations, the work was cosmetic in nature, and this well-known architect seems to have made little lasting impression on the building. What changes he did make appear to have been largely erased during the reconstruction of the 1920s.

When the Duke family purchased Rough Point in 1922, it was then thirty-one years old, and styles had changed. The house did not meet their needs either in size or floorplan, and they hired Horace Trumbauer to make suitable modifications. The Dukes' connection with Trumbauer was an old one. Their New York house was one of his earlier projects, and they had also commissioned him to design a palatial house that was never completed at their New Jersey estate. Outside of his work for the Dukes, Trumbauer's firm was very active in Newport, and several houses from his drawing board still survive, including Clarendon Court, Miramar, and The Elms.

It was Trumbauer who had the greatest lasting effect on the interior of the house. Under his direction and with the firm of White Allom as interior decorators, the floorplan and aesthetics of the house changed substantially. The wooden floors and much of the dark oak tracery and paneling popular during the Victorian era gave way to marble floors and molded plaster ceilings that provided a lighter look more in keeping with the decor of the 1920s. The dining room and the stairway were enlarged, and a new drawing room and spacious music room were added. Several new guest rooms were installed above the music room, and this new wing extended the northeast end of the house by sixty feet. On the exterior Trumbauer used materials identical to the original construction. Only careful examination reveals where the original ends and the new work begins. Although she lived here longer than anyone else, Doris Duke never changed the substance of her parents' alterations. She enjoyed fine-tuning the decoration and details throughout her life, but regarded the structure itself as a finished work.

Rough Point was occupied as a part-time residence for one hundred and four years, which in terms of Newport's lengthy history may not seem a lot, but is in fact a longer period than for many of the largest houses in Newport. The original design resonated with every owner and every architect, and throughout its history all have carefully preserved this American vision of an English manor by the seaside.

James B. "Buck" Duke, and Doris, circa 1913.

6

Families of Rough Point

For 104 years Rough Point was a very private residence situated in one of the most beautiful locations in Rhode Island. Aside from its staff and its guests, only three families have enjoyed strolling on its rolling lawn and waking up to its surf and sunrises. Frederick and Louise Vanderbilt were not only the first of these families, but also the creators of Rough Point, and their vision still dominates the landscape. They were followed by the Leeds and the Dukes, but it was the last resident, Doris Duke, who gave the house the character for which it will always be known.

Frederick Vanderbilt was the seventh child of William Vanderbilt and the grandson of Cornelius Vanderbilt, who founded the family fortune. Always a loyal participant in the family business, Frederick grew up as a younger son in a financial empire that passed its money and power to elder sons. It seems to have suited the retiring Frederick to remain a smaller part of the larger Vanderbilt dynasty. Nonetheless, Vanderbilts were synonymous with grand architecture, and Frederick constructed no less than three great houses by the time he died. Besides Rough Point, there was a town house in New York and the house that he cherished the most, his estate in Hyde Park, New York. It was there that he retired to beautiful views of the Hudson Valley and his beloved library. As an inheritor of great wealth, he was one of a very select group of heirs who was careful and clever enough to die with more money than he inherited. His quiet lifestyle, as well as a lack of children, did not promote lavish spending like that of his siblings and may well have been a reason that he did not relish Newport with the same intensity as his siblings. Although he enjoyed and participated in Rough Point's construction, he only spent a few summers there before renting it out and eventually selling it.

William Leeds, known as the tinplate king, was at the height of his wealth in 1908, and his wife Nancy desired a house in Newport to complete her social aspirations. When the Vanderbilts offered Rough Point for sale, Leeds purchased it promptly. The Leeds's ambitions were not to be realized, however, as Mr. Leeds suffered a series of strokes resulting in his death in 1910. For the next dozen years, Mrs. Leeds spent less time in the house, and more and more time in Europe, eventually marrying Prince Christopher of Greece. In 1922, needing money, she sold the house to James Duke thus starting Rough Point's most illustrious era.

Doris and Nanaline: This photograph is believed to have been taken on a family trip to France in 1923.

Doris and Alletta: The photograph at left shows the two girls with their trophies for a "Sand Modeling Contest" at Bailey's Beach in 1924. Just out of the photograph is the entry itself, a rather shapeless circle of sand and seaweed. The trophy that Doris won is part of the collections at Rough Point along with a number of others for tennis, dancing, and similar activities.

One of Doris Duke's steadfast childhood friends was Alletta Morris whose family also owned a house in Newport. Alletta's childhood diary is in the possession of the Preservation Society of Newport County and provides not only an invaluable record of children's activities during the 1920s, but also the only known insight into Doris Duke's activities at a young age.

In the late-19th century, James Buchanan "Buck" Duke took his father's successful tobacco business and built it into one of the first national monopolies and one of the largest fortunes of its day. In the process, he moved from North Carolina to New York and married an eligible Atlanta widow named Nanaline Holt Inman. Their only child, Doris, was born in 1912. Nanaline was enamored of Newport, and in 1915 the Dukes started vacationing there, renting a succession of houses until they purchased Rough Point. The Dukes' renovations at Rough Point were complete in 1924, but the family had little time to enjoy them, since Buck Duke died in 1925. Doris Duke was devoted to her father, and his death was a major blow to her at the age of thirteen. It was a loss that affected her for the rest of her life.

Throughout her teenage years, Doris spent her summers at Rough Point but in 1935 she married Jimmy Cromwell, and during and after her marriage, Newport was only a tangential part of her life. Nanaline continued her summers at Rough Point through 1938, but in September of that year one of the worst hurricanes in New England's history devastated Rhode Island. Rough Point was not spared, with winds and flooding that tore apart the landscape, although the house remained largely undamaged. This event, and World War II soon after,

Doris went occasionally to Rough Point in the fifties, a time that the house was little used. This photograph is one of a series in her personal collections that documented a trip to Rough Point for what appears to have been a picnic on the terrace. Other photos in the group seem to indicate that the house was shuttered and mothballed.

curtailed Mrs. Duke's visits. After the war, advancing age tended to keep her time at the house brief and infrequent, and by the early fifties the house was empty but for its part-time caretakers.

Doris, then in her forties, was at first unsure what to do with her mother's house. Many of Newport's large summer houses were more or less abandoned, ghostly relics of another age. An offer by Miss Duke to donate Rough Point to Newport Hospital met with little interest, and the fate of the property hung in the balance. By the late 1950s, her thinking had changed, and it is clear that her enthusiasm for the house was growing. Photographs of the house from that period show that it was sparsely furnished, and in 1958 and 1959 she started purchasing art and antiques to fill it. In 1962, the house was reopened and over the years became one of her favorites. By the end of her life, she spent as much time there as she did in any other of her residences.

Once so private, Rough Point now shares its wonders, but the house is more than just objects and scenery. It fascinates because it reveals the character of its owners in the work and the creativity that they wrought upon it, and it is through their choices that this house remains so vibrant today.

Once she had made the decision to make Rough Point her summer residence, Doris Duke purchased some major art works and furnishings even before she moved in. Antique Chinese wallpaper, 16th-century tapestries, and a painting by Renoir were parts of her plan for the house.

Rough Point's Landscape

In 1887, upon the recommendation of his friend, Seward Webb, Frederick Vanderbilt hired Frederick Law Olmsted to design the new grounds at Rough Point. The Boston-based landscape architect was well known by 1887; his designs for New York's Central Park, the Boston Park System, and numerous Newport summer cottages, spoke for themselves, and his vision of the American landscape and its practical interpretation set seminal trends in the 19th century that are still influential today. Despite the obvious attraction of an Olmsted landscape for Vanderbilt's new property, the cost for implementing the original plan was too high and the features too ambitious for the relatively small size of the estate, so the project was scaled down several times. Initially, the landscape was to include barns, stables and other outbuildings, even a bowling alley, set amidst a landscape designed in the style of an English park. In the final draft Olmsted created a vision that highlighted the rugged beauty of the site with its remarkable ocean vistas.

The work progressed, and by 1889 more than 34,000 plants were ordered and installed at Rough Point. The site was overplanted to be sure, but Olmsted knew that many plants would be lost under the harsh conditions of a landscape by the sea, and those that remained would serve as a windbreak and support for each other. In the first season, as a temporary measure, fast-growing squash plants were planted over large expanses of lawn to hide the freshly turned earth resulting from re-grading, leading local wags to dub the new estate "Pumpkin Lawn" in its early years.

By 1891, with the house and grounds complete, Rough Point was described by critics as "an attractive mixture of luxury and rustic simplicity," giving the impression of a "picturesque manor house of the English shires." Sweeping lawns accentuated the rough terrain, while thickly planted shrubberies screened the property from its neighbors and deepened its spacious quality. Throughout the property, views to the water were shaped and accentuated by carefully placed specimen trees or small groves.

After the Leeds family bought Rough Point in 1908, Mr. Leeds only enjoyed the property for two years before his death. Subsequently Rough Point was used only infrequently by his wife and often rented, so little attention was paid to the grounds. In 1922, after thirty years of irregular occupancy of the estate, only the hardiest of Olmsted's plants survived.

When the Dukes purchased the estate, they brought considerable experience in shaping landscapes. Gardeners from Mr. Duke's vast New Jersey estate, Duke Farms, were brought to

Frederick Law Olmsted defined landscape architecture in the United States during the 19th century. Noted for many important and monumental works including Central Park in New York City and the "Emerald Ring" of parks in Boston, Olmsted was also responsible for the landscaping of many private Newport homes, including Rough Point.

F. L. & J. C. OLMSTED,
LANDSCAPE ARCHITECTS,
BROOKLINE, MASS.

Planting and order list for *F. W. Vanderbilt Esq.*
Newport R.I.

Date, ...

No. on Plan.	NAME OF PLANT.	Quantity Ordered.	Quantity Received.	Size & Condition Ordered.	Where Ordered.	Condition.	Spacing.
33	Vaccinum Pennsylvanicum	50					1
34	Daphne cneorum	40		extra	Meyer		
35	Viburnum Lantana	10			Dorchmier		
36	Crataegus Crus-galli	3			Dorchmier		15.
37							
38	Stuartia pentagyna	32		2-3'	Pimple		3
39	Rhus Osbeckii	12			Dorchmier		
40	Hedera Helix	200		3 y strong	Dorchmier 25 Pimple		1-2
41	Forsythia Fortunei	18		large	Ross		
42	Cydonia Japonica	18			Stokes		
43	Lonicera Xylosteum	15	✓	large	Ross		
44	Calycanthus floridus	20	✓	4-5-2 yrs	Thuson	EHB	
45	Philadelphus	50	✓	large	Moon		
	Ampelopsis quinquefolia	50		"	Pimple+B.		

The document above from the Olmsted Archives illustrates the extensive plan by Olmsted for the new plantings in 1889. Detailed instructions, along with the design plan, enabled the gardeners to follow the architect's plan precisely.

Newport to oversee improvements. The house's terraces were redesigned, and the extensive shrubberies along Bellevue Avenue were thickened to increase privacy. The driveway turnaround, which had been laid out in a teardrop design by Olmsted, was enlarged into a broader circle to complement the enlarged scale of the house.

The broad sweeping lawns, which captured views to the water and the rocky shoreline, remained an integral part of Rough Point's landscape, as they do today. Privet hedges were planted to protect a large cut flower garden and a vegetable garden from the fierce ocean winds. These gardens were located far from the main house and, even today, function as separate and distinct garden "rooms," which are not connected in any form to the views or setting of the main house.

One of the most profound landscaping events in local history transformed Rough Point and all of Newport when a powerful hurricane in September of 1938 tore apart decades of careful work. In the following years Mrs. Duke's attendance fell off, and Rough Point saw little more than routine maintenance. Even so, during this period the sides of the ravine were planted heavily with rock garden plants and low shrubs, and Rugosa rose hedges edged the lawns and softened the wire fence that was installed to discourage intrusions from the Cliff Walk.

When Doris Duke took up residence in the house, the landscaping was refreshed, although she chose not to make major changes, leaving the property largely as it is today. Many remnants of the original Olmsted plan are still in evidence. The large oak that frames the view to the water at the main entrance may predate the Vanderbilts, and the thick belt of low plantings near the front wall are also original. In the 1960s Miss Duke added rhododendron, lilacs, dogwoods, yews and junipers. The yews along the front of the main house were pruned carefully to appear as picturesque and windswept as the site itself.

Arch at Rough Point, Cliff Walk, Newport, R. I.

Flowers for the cutting garden were started from seed in the greenhouses at Duke Farms. They were transported to Newport in mid-May each year and set out in the geometric beds of the garden. Snapdragons, begonias, geraniums, dahlias, marigolds, petunias, cosmos and gladiolas were some of Miss Duke's favorites. Beds of iris, lilies and roses remained from earlier days. Sheltered from the wind, the long row of peach trees produced fruit every season. These trees provided both a practical and decorative accent to the garden.

The grounds of Rough Point have been maintained by Duke family gardeners since 1922, and their work has always taken the form of an epic campaign. The qualities that make Rough Point so picturesque often spell trouble for its staff. The site is rough and rocky, with soils thin enough to barely keep its grass green. Throughout the twentieth century, numerous hurricanes and merciless winter weather battered and beat this rocky peninsula, making spring replanting a major annual task. Despite its gardeners' best efforts to tame it, ultimately it is the rustic simplicity, first established by Olmsted and Vanderbilt, that has remained the true spirit behind its landscape.

One of the site's most notable original features was a stone bridge that arched across the ravine in front of the house. It solved Vanderbilt's problem of what to do with the heavy foot-traffic on the Cliff Walk every summer, and at the same time, provided a picturesque icon for the house itself. Indeed, early photographs of the house almost always feature the house and the bridge together. The sculptural quality of the bridge was ever-changing as the tide rose and fell in the ravine, the surf sometimes ferocious and at other times almost flat. At the 1891 housewarming, the bridge and the chasm were artfully illuminated, a celebration of the "rustic simplicity" of the landscape design. Sadly, the original bridge was swept away in the 1938 hurricane and has been replaced ever since with a succession of wooden bridges. The rocks forming the ravine comprise the actual geographical feature known as Rough Point, a name that predates the house by many years and goes back perhaps as far as the 18th century. The larger rock formation to the south, often mistakenly referred to as Rough Point is actually named Midship Rock.

The Great Hall

The Great Hall is one of the many areas of the house that Horace Trumbauer changed for James and Nanaline Duke. In its original configuration, the room had approximately the same square footage as today, but part of the ceiling reached all the way to the rafters—about fifteen feet higher than the current ceiling height. Also, the Hall featured more architectural details, such as small balconies and oriel windows, to give it the feeling of a palatial courtyard. Even the bedroom of Mrs. Vanderbilt had a diminutive balcony overlooking the Hall, and the third floor rooms at either end were separated by the space in the center and were reached by separate stairways from each end of the second floor.

The Dukes clearly wanted their home at Rough Point to serve as much as a display space for their fine art collection as an architectural tour de force. The ceiling is now at the second-floor level throughout, and the molded plaster detail is likely all from the Trumbauer renovation. At twenty-six feet, the height of the ceiling is inspiring. The Dukes installed the bright marble floor in this room, which had originally been built with dark oak floors to match the woodwork. The doors and paneling are remnants of the Vanderbilts' design, but the overall amount of oak and some of the detailing was changed with Trumbauer's reinterpretation of the space. The art on view includes some of the best pieces in the collection, befitting such a grand setting. The arrangement of the room is just as it was when Doris Duke was last in residence.

The group of three tapestries is the best in the house, and each probably retains its original size and borders. Made in about 1510, the tapestries are illustrations of contemporary courtly life, including a courting scene, a betrothal scene in the large central panel, and a coronation scene. The coronation is thought to be that of Louis XII, a French monarch of the period who was much beloved by his people.

Many of the paintings in Rough Point were created by artists who painted for the royal court. First in the Great Hall is *Gentleman in a Red Coat*, by Henry Raeburn (1756–1823), an 18th-century limner to royalty in Scotland. Although the gentleman is unidentified, his clothing and noble bearing help to convey his importance in contemporary society. An exquisitely charming *Lady in a Blue Cloak* was painted by Ferdinand Bol (1616–1680), a colleague of Rembrandt's in Amsterdam during the 17th century, who developed his own elegant style. The portrait of this young beauty reflects some of Rembrandt's style and quiet expression of elegance. Two large

The Ming dynasty in China was the dawn of a new era in porcelain decoration. A new technique known as Fa Hua utilized the placement of tiny threads of clay on the surface of a piece, to prevent the glaze from sagging and blending together in the kiln. Although there were only three basic glaze colors usually used together at the time —deep blue, azure and ochre—the new design development meant that intricate designs could be successfully executed. The central piece in the Great Hall is a wine jar that is also pierced, greatly increasing the difficulty of finishing the piece without allowing it to collapse. Fittingly, the subject of the decoration is the mythical wise immortals, surrounded by symbols of their intelligence and longevity.

(Right) Sir Anthony van Dyck's double portrait,
The Earl of Newport and Lord Goring,
is one of the masterpieces of the Rough Point
collection, but it also represents an intriguing story
of the English civil war. The two noblemen were
the closest of friends, and held high offices on the
Royalist side during the conflict. However, Goring
vacillated in his allegiance and was subsequently
mistrusted by both sides. Following the war, van
Dyck painted two versions of the painting for the
two friends. Despite Goring's calm appearance in
the painting, he was soon forced to flee to France,
then Spain. This painting was probably his copy,
and eventually made its way from Spain to a sale
in America.

————— ✠ —————

(Opp. Page) Portrait of Raphael Franco, Sir
Thomas Gainsborough (1727-1788), England;
oil on canvas, dated 1781. This portrait of the
preoccupied Italian gentleman was painted in the
same year as the artist's famous portraits of George
III and his queen.

portraits by Thomas Gainsborough (1727-1788) show the accomplished and graceful style of the most versatile English painter of the 18th century. His portraits of Lord Peter Burrell and Raphael Franco were added to the collection by Doris Duke and her father, respectively. Both portraits convey something of the character of the subjects, while the backgrounds are idealized landscapes; Burrell's background is a pleasant and peaceful woodland, in contrast to Franco's urban landscape, with the prominent dome of St. Paul's Cathedral anchoring the scene.

An assembled pair of portraits in the Hall are Charles II, in the style of Jan Mijtens (1614-1670), and his queen, Henrietta Maria, in the style of John Michael Wright (1617-1694). These pictures were placed in matching frames many decades ago to form a pleasing 17th-century couple and the appearance of a matched pair of portraits. The queen's portrait is similar to one painted by van Dyck. A gem from the 17th century is a double portrait by Sir Anthony van Dyck (1599-1641), depicting the Earl of Newport and his good friend, Lord Goring. The artist

was one of the most important and prolific portraitists of the 17th century, who spent two years early in his career in the studio of Peter Paul Rubens. In 1632 he came to London as the chief court painter to King Charles I. The Earl of Newport and Lord Goring were friends and leaders during the English civil war, though it was discovered that Goring was accepting funds from both sides in the conflict, causing his eventual flight to Europe. Two diminutive but exquisite art works are the portraits of the Duke d'Alençon and Diane de Poitiers, from the studio of the French royal court painter, François Clouet (1515-1572). Clouet served four French kings, and his studio produced these highly detailed portraits along with genre scenes and even decorations for funeral ceremonies and the triumphal entries of the French kings.

Chinese porcelains comprise a second category of art works in the Great Hall, and Doris Duke assembled some rare examples of these. There are three garden seats and three wine jars, all in the style of the Ming Dynasty of about 1475. Although only a few glaze colors were used by these Ming artisans, the style and beauty of these pieces is striking and was made possible by an innovative contemporary process known as Fa Hua, which keeps the glazes from running together during firing.

The prize among the porcelain pieces in the Great Hall is a highly decorated wine jar that incorporated yet another step before the initial firing. When the vessel had been formed by the artist and dried to the stage at which it could support itself, hundreds of small bits of the

The unknown young beauty in a blue shawl is a favorite among visitors to Rough Point, and the painting is a gem of late Renaissance portraiture from Holland. The artist, Ferdinand Bol (1616-1680), was a student in Rembrandt's studio in Amsterdam before becoming one of the city's leading painters. He developed his own style, combining Rembrandt's quiet expression of character with greater color and elegance. Lady in a Blue Cloak is a figure in peaceful repose, and a superb example of the subtle changes of light and shadow that characterized this period of Dutch painting. Especially well executed and preserved without substantial alteration, this painting is one of the finest in the house.

Portrait of Diane de Poitiers and Portrait of the Duke d'Alençon, studio of François Clouet (1515-1572), France; oil on panel. The artist's studio produced numerous copies of his portraits of royal and noble luminaries for purchase by their admirers.

background were cut away, leaving a pierced outer shell for the jar, with a light and elegant appearance. As many as seventy separate steps might be involved in the production of this style of porcelain. The design itself consists of purely decorative bands at the top and bottom, and in the middle, scenes of the Immortals paying homage to Shou-Lao, the god of longevity. The god is surrounded by symbols of long life, including flying cranes and a crawling tortoise.

The premier bronze in the Great Hall is *The Sleeping Putto*, by Flemish sculptor François Du Quesnoy (1597-1643). In the period 1625-1630 the artist explored the motifs of the young child,

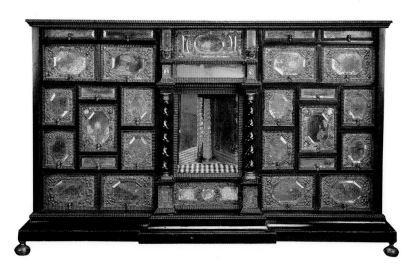

including cupids, satyrs and bacchantes, as well as simple putti, such as the one at Rough Point. These pieces were some of his most famous and influential sculptures. This figure of a sleeping child is reminiscent of decorations found on ancient sarcophagi, which the artist studied during a residency of several years in Italy.

Sleeping Putto, François Duquesnoy (1597-1643), circa 1630, southern Netherlands; bronze. The artist sculpted many similar tender and sensual statuettes and reliefs, in both marble and bronze.

—— ✠ ——

(Left) Table chest, unknown maker, circa 17th century, Spain; ebony and secondary woods, brass, glass, semiprecious brilliants. This highly decorated storage piece includes a playful trompe l'oeil receding chamber in the center and richly detailed trim.

—— ✠ ——

(Opposite) Courting Scene, Brussels, Gothic tapestry, circa 1510, Flanders; silk and wool. This central panel in a group of three richly illustrates the contemporary social life of royalty and nobility.

19

The Yellow Room

Louis XVI style mantel clock by an unknown maker, Paris, France, circa 1775; steel, bronze, ormolu.

The Yellow Room is a striking contrast to the Great Hall, which precedes it in a walk through Rough Point. In fact, all the central rooms on the first floor are similar in feeling, with marble or dark wood floors, stone and dark oak trim, and high ceilings. Entering the Yellow Room is like looking at a page in a decoration pattern book of the late-19th century. The classical design elements of this room were in vogue at the time and published in various books, not least of which was *The Decoration of Houses* by Edith Wharton and Ogden Codman. The efforts that created this room make it one of the prettiest in the house, and one whose elegant beauty never fails to elicit praise. The height of the ceiling is attenuated by the presence of a large rock crystal chandelier and the white classical trim, all of which stand out against the yellow walls. Straight across the room is a George III fireplace, done in contrasting dark red and white marble. Although the floor is dark, it is a parquet de Versailles in French oak of 18th-century vintage, and a great find that is typical of Doris Duke's collecting.

House staff remember that the Yellow Room received only little use, serving mostly as a passage to the Music Room and the Solarium. It is a pretty picture of a room, in keeping with the ideas from the pattern books. Miss Duke found the furnishings and garnitures piece by piece to create a complete and personal assemblage of the finest quality.

Adorning the mantel is a group of objects carefully chosen for their aesthetic design and subtle, elegant colors. At the center is a clock made in Paris about 1775, in the Louis XVI style; a figure of Wisdom sits astride the drum-shaped case that holds the clockworks, all done in gilt bronze. On each side of the clock are Louis XVI urn-shaped scent vessels of carved alabaster and gilt bronze. The top of each vessel can be turned upside-down to expose a small amount of scent, to be wafted through the air. At the ends of the mantel are a pair of Paris jardinières of about 1810, decorated with bands of gilt and painted in black and tones of gray with scenes of cupids and nymphs.

A small and incidental piece in the artfully contrived Yellow Room, the terracotta sculpture, Nymph and Child is nonetheless an intimate and dynamic work of art. Attributed to the French sculptor known as Clodion (Claude Michel, 1738-1814), this group is typical of his work that often featured nymphs, satyrs, bacchantes and other classical figures sensually portrayed. While his earlier figures were often shown in energetic, whirling motion, later pieces such as this one reflect long, flowing lines and a restrained tone. Executed in great detail, the nymph carries a pitcher, with a basket of fruit on her head, while the child at her side holds a staff draped with clusters of grapes.

Giltwood and glass door panels, designed by Lorenzo da Ferrari (1686-1744), Genoa, Italy; wood, mirrored glass and gold leaf. These ornate doors are in the rococo style, each with a sphinx and classical figures among scrolling strapwork and foliate borders.

Louis XVI style open arm chair attributed to Falconet, France; wood, silk, paint and gold leaf. Part of a set with three other chairs and a sofa, this piece exemplifies Doris Duke's collector's eye for rare furnishings and textiles.

At the west side of the room are groupings of remarkable objects: two pairs of mirrored doors, and a pair of unusual Russian tables. The gilt wood and glass doors were made in Genoa during the 18th century, and originally graced one of the city's fine palaces. The architect Stanford White purchased and imported them for the William Whitney mansion in New York. They were not used in that project and remained in White's warehouse until after his death, when they were sold. Doris Duke bought the four panels at the Bois Doré estate auction in Newport, in 1977. These are, however, only half of the original doors. The remainder reside at the Metropolitan Museum of Art in New York. The tables were made of ivory and silver in the late-18th century and are the only Russian pieces in the house. The two tables are slightly different in decoration, the top corners of one inlaid with rosettes, and the second inlaid with the monogram of Catherine the Great. These were purchased by Doris Duke during her residence in Paris.

Perhaps the most astonishing pieces in the Yellow Room are the suite of Louis XVI chairs and sofa, made in the mid-18th century. Several of the pieces are stamped "Falconet." Originally used in the Château de Valency, this group was bought by Doris Duke in 1960, while she was still in the initial stages of redecorating Rough Point. The elaborately carved areas retain their

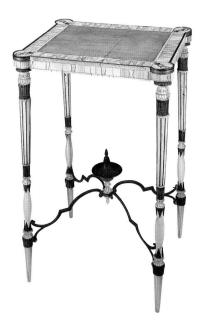

Neoclassical style occasional table by an unknown maker, circa 1790, Russia; ivory, wood and silver. As it would have originally appeared with some ivory inlay dyed a vibrant blue, and with sparkling silver, it befitted the royal monogram of Catherine the Great, inlaid in the four corners of the top.

The 18th century portraitist John Hoppner was a favorite of the Duke family. Like most of the artists represented in the collection, he was a painter to the royal court and a master portraitist of his time. Portrait of Lady St. John shows the master's hand in his delicate and glowing rendition of the lady's face and hair, the delicacy of her gown, and the elegance of the setting. The Rough Point collection includes three other works by Hoppner.

original green paint and gold leaf, but even more extraordinary is the original embroidered silk upholstery. The fabric is so fragile that it also provides evidence that this room was rarely used but was instead seen as a delightful image of artistry and decoration. The central carpet is also French, an Aubusson of the late-18th century, with griffins, urns and cameos with floral garlands.

Complementing the furnishings, which are mostly French, are several English portraits, continuing the trend of English portraiture throughout the house. Over the mantel is a striking portrait of Lady Fitzroy, by John Hoppner, probably painted not long before her death in 1797. On the west wall of the room hangs another Hoppner, this one of Lady St. John, also displaying all the expertise of the foremost English portraitist of his time. Also on the west wall is a portrait of Thomas Edward Freeman, painted in the late-18th century by Prince Hoare, an English painter and writer. On the south wall is a portrait of an unidentified lady, done in the style of Gainsborough, and a portrait of Master Thomas Barber, painted about 1800 by another royal painter, Sir Thomas Lawrence. Lawrence followed van Dyck, Gainsborough, Reynolds and Hoppner— all represented in the Rough Point collection—as the preeminent portrait painter in Britain.

The Music Room

The largest addition to Rough Point by the Duke family in 1922 was the wing to the east, which included the Music Room on the ground floor. This is a large space decorated by Doris Duke with art and antiques carefully sought over decades. The Chinese hand-painted wallpaper was created in the 18th century and is composed of two separate sets of panels. The subtle blue and green tones of the paper and surrounding trim is complemented by the warm gold of the silk curtains, which in turn pick up the gilt ornamentation on the furniture. When the curtains are open, the blue sea and green grass create a natural connection to the room.

The current decoration of the Music Room was an ongoing project of Doris Duke's. By the late 1950s, her mother, who had traditionally used Rough Point as her summer place, had become elderly and frail and resided solely at the Stanhope Hotel in New York. Miss Duke visited Rough Point with friends to look over the house and consider additions to the décor. Some areas of the house were not heavily furnished, and in 1958 and 1959 she bought separate lots of the Chinese wallpaper at auction, and these were installed in special removable panels in the Music Room. The trim was painted the subtle green and gold tones that still adorn it today. Furniture and ceramics were collected and interchanged over the decades, and the quarter-sawn oak floor was replaced with the 18th-century French floor about thirty years ago. Some of the furniture—that at the west end of the room—was for display only, while the grouping near the fireplace was created for small gatherings before or after dinner. Staff at Rough Point recall Elizabeth Taylor reclining on one of the sofas to ease her aching back, and visiting musicians playing jazz on the piano.

The far end of the room is a carefully crafted assemblage, offering the visitor a vista of fine French furnishings and exquisite Chinese porcelains in a unique setting. The floor is antique French oak, in the parquet de Versailles style, from an 18th-century house near Paris. The clock that dominates the wall is in the Louis XVI style, built of carved and gilded wood, with the spring-powered works located in the center of the sunburst. The carpets include a French Savonnerie floral rug from the early-19th century in front of the fireplace, a silk, silver and gold East Turkestan Kashgar of about 1800 near the piano, and a Bessarabian kilim at the west end. All of these delicate pieces show the care that Doris Duke took, not only in finding antiques and

When Doris Duke began her purchases for Rough Point embellishments in 1958, she found some beautiful Chinese wallpaper. Almost two years later, at the end of 1959, she bought another group of panels, different in design, but still similar in color and style to the earlier set.

The paper shown here features large blossoming peony trees, with exotic birds, butterflies and Oriental vessels. Each panel is more than eleven feet tall, while the scenes vary in width, according to the space on the wall where they were installed. When the curtains are open, the blue and green hues of the wallpaper seem to combine with the blue of the ocean and green of the lawns to create a large, fantastic and colorful landscape.

A whimsical and charming piece, this piano stool portrays one of the traditional symbols of Newport, the scallop shell, in its beautifully carved seat. Made in Italy by an unknown cabinetmaker, it dates to the mid-18th century.

Far grander is the suite of Louis XVI chairs and sofa with original illustrative upholstery from about 1780; this one features a tale of a bat, a duck and a bush, and also a story of a dog becoming jealous of his reflection in the water.

choosing the best examples, but also the concern she had for their cleaning, support and mending over the years, in much the same way as a good museum cares for collections.

One of the gems of the Music Room is the set of Louis XVI chairs, with original pictorial upholstery illustrating fables of the French storyteller, La Fontaine. Some of the tales include "The Lion's Share," "The Fox and the Crane," and "The Crow and the Pitcher," all offering moral advice through the animals' adventures. There are twelve chairs in the set, and a settee, each with different scenes on the seat and back. It may be surprising that such formal and elegant furniture would be covered with scenes filled with bats, mice and other creatures, but it was the height of fashion in the late-18th century. As with some other furnishings throughout the house, Doris Duke found examples with near-perfect paint, gilt and surviving original upholstery.

To the north side of the room, a Steinway and Sons grand piano fills the alcove created for the purpose. When the Dukes purchased the house the piano may have been largely ornamental, but after 1962, the Steinway here was used almost every day by its owner, although it was still secondary in use to the piano in the Pine Room. Flanking the piano's alcove are two masterpieces of French furniture, a pair of Louis XVI ebony and lacquer commodes, bedecked with gilt bronze fittings and red marble tops. The lacquer on these pieces is built up in layers of different colors, and then carved for a three-dimensional effect and contrast of color as well. Though these are 19th-century versions of an earlier style, the artisans' work rivals that of the original masters.

Among the furniture are carefully arranged some of Doris Duke's best Chinese porcelain pieces in the house. In a room as large and artfully arranged as this, most pieces blend in to become part of the harmonious whole; yet two remarkable mid-18th century Qianlong jars standing more than four feet high flank the fireplace. A variety of other, smaller Qianlong famille rose pieces stand along the walls and throughout the room. And finally anchoring the south side of the room are another superb set of three Kangxi famille verte jars of about 1700.

At each door to the Music Room is a console table holding an 18th-century, gilt bronze musical automaton. These bejeweled pieces are made in the form of pagodas, topped by ostriches, hung with prisms, decorated with paste brilliants, and standing on feet in the form of elephants. Probably made by John Cox in England, these were produced for the Indian market and fit nicely in the oriental theme set by the wallpaper and porcelains. Flanking the automaton on the north side is the only Japanese porcelain in the room, a wonderful pair of Kakiemon candlesticks, formed as bamboo stems resting on shishi mask tripod bases.

(Above) Central in this scene is one of a pair of George III ormolu musical automatons. It plays a variety of tunes, which can be chosen by turning a jeweled flower. As the music plays, tropical ocean scenes painted on a strip of paper pass behind a ship in the front. The candlestick—one of a pair—is among the few Japanese pieces in the collection; these rare ceramic pieces are Kakiemon style (17th-18th centuries) with shishi masks forming the bases. (Left) In the alcove of the Music Room stand a Steinway concert grand piano and a 19th century French harp.

The Morning Room

Despite its name, the Morning Room was usually used as a sitting room after dinner. The Duke family may have kept the earlier designation for this room, but after they added the Solarium to Rough Point, the latter was the obvious choice for morning activities. This room, more than most, emulates the English Tudor period, and Doris Duke furnished the room with furniture and artworks in keeping with that theme. As in many houses in Newport, decorative elements in Rough Point are taken from much older European houses. In this room the deep brown paneling combines some early elements with later woodwork. One of the original panels above the fireplace bears two sets of initials, along with an armorial device and the date 1623. A carved frieze above the main panels includes scrolling foliage and a mythical beast with a large mouth and a long, curling nose. The ceiling, an installation by the Duke family in 1922, is highly decorated with molded plaster elements, featuring portraits of Alexander the Great and other classical heroes placed in ornamental medallions.

Above the sofa on the east side of the room is one of Doris Duke's favorite works of art and her last major purchase for Rough Point. The title of this marine landscape by Jan van de Cappelle (1624-1679) leaves nothing to the imagination: *A Visit of the Stadtholder Prince Frederick Hendrick to the Fleet of the States General at Dordrecht in 1646*. The scene evokes little of the pomp and grandeur of the title, instead depicting a still, sultry day, with ships drying their sails in the diffuse light of a midsummer sky, amid subdued activity on the quays. The painting retains its original 17th-century frame, heavily carved and decoratively inlaid. It's a very rare survivor of the period; later tastes usually replaced old frames with the now-pervasive ornately carved and gold-leafed varieties.

Portrait of Mrs. Hays, *Sir Joshua Reynolds (1723-1792), England; oil on canvas, circa mid-18th century. Reynolds became painter to the king in 1784, following many years of painting accomplished portraits conveying calm dignity and realistic portrayal of character.*

If there was any doubt that Doris Duke had a sense of humor, the small pillows embroidered with mottoes show that she was willing to poke fun at herself. A pillow in one of the bedrooms reads, "Be reasonable… do it my way." Two pillows in the morning room suggest, "Familiarity breeds," and "My decision is maybe, and that's final." Finally, a prankster placed signs on two new Jeeps for the Duke Farms security department, reading, "Duke Farms Fuzz;" and Doris Duke thought it was so funny she decided to keep the signs on the vehicles for several months.

An anecdote about the Morning Room relates Doris Duke's preference for warm temperatures. The fireplaces in the house are all functional, and in most cases were laid with enormous piles of wood. They were always kept ready to light, an operation that she insisted on doing herself, and are laid as they were the last time that she was in residence. The Morning Room was a favorite sitting area after dinner, and the guests discovered just how warm it had become when they found the after-dinner chocolates on the coffee table completely melted from the heat of the roaring fire.

Visit of the Stadtholder Prince Frederick
Hendrick to the Fleet of the States
General at Dordrecht in 1646, *Jan van de
Cappelle (1624-1679), The Netherlands, oil on
canvas, circa 1648. A merchant by trade and a
painter only by avocation, van de Cappelle is
nonetheless recognized as one of the foremost
marine artists of his day.*

Other art works in the room reinforce the emphasis on English
art in the house. Portraits include: *Mrs. Sarah Amsinck*, attributed to Sir
Joshua Reynolds (circa 1770); the striking and sensitive *Portrait of Mrs.
Hays*, painted by Reynolds; and the charming *Portrait of a Lady in a Red
Cloak*, circle of Joseph Highmore (circa mid–18th century). Literally
in the midst of these portraits is an Italianate painting in the style of
Salvatore Rosa, depicting an estuary filled with ships in a romantic
landscape. Other rare pieces include items that convey Doris Duke's
interest in exceptional historic textiles: three needlework pictures of the 17th century depict
a Biblical scene, images of royalty, and a romantic scene. In the style of the day, the frames of
these delightful pictures are covered in ornamental tortoiseshell. Her taste in textiles extended to
magnificent carpets located throughout the house; one of the foundations for the decoration of
the Morning Room is an exquisite pair of 17th-century Portuguese needlework carpets.

The Morning Room furnishings are English, with a few notable exceptions. There are
two sets of Dutch rococo side chairs (circa 18th century), with scrolling backs and seat rails.
Their ornate shapes are bedecked with marquetry images of classical urns and mythical figures.
These chairs contrast sharply with the subdued English furniture and are further distinguished
by brilliant yellow silk damask upholstery. Another European piece is a South German baroque
walnut fall-front desk, made in the early–18th century. The upper paneled doors reveal an
elaborate interior of pigeonholes, drawers, and a glazed cupboard. English furniture in the room
includes a variety of chairs, in Jacobean, William and Mary, and Queen Anne styles.

The three sofas are in the George III style, and are covered in reproduction fabrics. An oriental touch is found on the fireplace mantel, where four famille rose Chinese porcelain maidens (mid-18th century) watch over the room. There is a Guanyin Chinese mythical figure in the center, one of several in the house and an important part of Doris Duke's appreciation of Chinese art and culture.

The view from the south-facing windows is a dramatic glimpse of the Atlantic Ocean shore, though not as sweeping and grand as the views from the Solarium and Great Hall, with their larger groups of windows. Here can be found some evidence of Princess and Baby, the two Bactrian camels that once lived at Rough Point during the summers. On a hot summer day when the windows were open, one of the camels craned her neck into the room and nibbled on the loosely woven shades inside, leaving some slightly chewed areas that still remain. House staff recount that the camels would chew on just about anything they could reach, including some of the leaded windows on the house. That prompted Doris Duke to have slightly unattractive acrylic panels installed on every window, both to protect the house and to prevent the camels from poisoning themselves. It is an affectionate statement of Doris Duke's attitudes that when the needs of preservation or her collections conflicted with the animals, the animals were accommodated first.

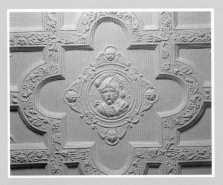

Molded plaster ceiling, Morning Room, Rough Point, circa 1924. Incorporated into the overall design of intersecting moldings are three styles of medallions, portraying Joshua, Hector and Alexander the Great.

—◄ ▣✦▣ ►—

Rococo style marquetry side chair, The Netherlands; walnut and various inlaid woods, 18th century. Each part of the chair, from leg to crest rail, is not only ornately shaped, but decoratively inlaid with foliage, urns and flowers.

The Grand Staircase

A major area of renovation at Rough Point from 1922 to 1924 was the main stairway. The original stairs ascended rather tightly to the second floor, but the Dukes wanted something more grand, and perhaps more befitting the English style of the house. Thus, a large bay was added to the front of the house to accommodate a straight flight of stairs up to a large and decorative landing and a parallel flight of stairs away from the front of the house to the second floor. The stairway itself roughly mimics English oak carvings, but two other elements are of equal importance. The large open space offered a perfect opportunity to show off an elaborate set of windows depicting the coats of arms of signers of the Magna Carta, and in the center, the arms of the Archbishop of Canterbury, the king, and the pope. Finally, the soaring walls in the staircase offered perfect backdrops for ancestral family portraits, as in an English country house. Lacking noble portraits of their own ancestors, the Dukes followed the lead of many of America's wealthiest families and shopped the world art market for masterpieces of European portraiture.

Ascending the stairs, one first encounters the young *King Charles II of England*, as painted by Sir Anthony van Dyck about 1640. The young king is resplendent in a highly ornamented suit and holding a walking stick. Following is the *Portrait of Mrs. Charlotte Dennison* painted by another royal painter, John Hoppner, in 1797. Far more regal is the *Portrait of Caroline, Duchess of Marlborough*, by English court painter Sir Joshua Reynolds, painted around 1780, probably in a setting at the family seat, Blenheim Castle. Next comes the *Portait of the Marchioness of Wellesley*, a famous French beauty of her day, shown with her two young sons about 1798. When the picture was painted it was sent to her husband, who was serving the British Empire in India. Toward the top of

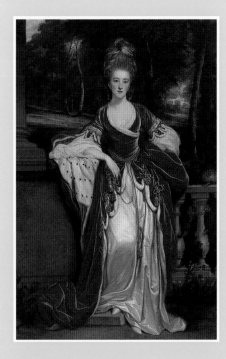

Portrait of Caroline, Duchess of Marlborough, *Sir Joshua Reynolds (1723-1792), England; oil on canvas, circa 1780. Grand and elegant portraits such as this one, with the duchess in her ceremonial garb, illustrate the rich formal style that brought the artist deserved recognition as the king's portraitist.*

✦━━❧❀❧━━✦

(Left) Queen Anne style settee, England; walnut, secondary woods with silk and wool fabrics; early-18th century. The elegant curves of the double-arch back and outscrolling arms of this piece are complemented by the upholstery fabric of illustrative petit point and gros point needlework.

Exploits of the Roman general, Scipio Africanus, *Flanders; silk and wool tapestry, late-16th century. Part of a group of four historical tapestries, this pictorial textile piece shows the great general conquering Carthage.*

the stairs, there is finally a Duke family picture, the *Portrait of Nanaline Holt Inman Duke*, painted by the English artist John Haslewood Shannon about 1905, not long before her marriage to James B. Duke. Beyond her mother's portrait is one of Doris Duke herself, painted by John Da Costa in 1924 when she was twelve. That was the year that the Dukes moved into Rough Point. These two paintings are the only likenesses of any family members in Rough Point, although a large number of photographs of family and friends have been gathered in a central archives at Duke Farms in New Jersey.

The hall at the base of the stairs was an area that received Doris Duke's attention in 1958, when she decided to make use of Rough Point after her mother no longer ventured to Newport in the summers. The Renaissance historical tapestries that cover the walls were bought for this room in that year: thus beginning Doris Duke's search for art works appropriate to Rough Point. The tapestries were made in Brussels in the late-16th century. They show important events in the career of the famous Roman general, Scipio Africanus (185–129 BC). Beginning with the tapestry under the stairs, one sees Roman soldiers besieging a city and a soldier with a battering ram attempting to break through a barricade; to the right of the Great Hall door is a scene of Scipio accepting the keys of the conquered Carthaginians; to the right of the Morning Room door is a scene of the Battle of Zama with the Roman troops of Scipio and the Carthaginian troops of Hannibal engaged in fierce combat; to the right of the Dining Room door there is a scene of Scipio receiving crowns and jewels.

A Queen Anne-style walnut settee sits between the two doors, and it exemplifies the simpler lines of the period (1702-1714). The lines of the legs are quite complex, but there is an elegance to the piercing in the stretchers. The rich upholstery fabric illustrates Doris Duke's intense interest in elaborate textiles. On the west side one sees a 17th-century English oak refectory table, with a waved frieze inlaid with alternating light and dark bands, on baluster-turned legs joined by a stretcher. On the table is a cloisonné enamel and gilt metal cylindrical tripod censer made in China in the 18th century, with a decoration of stylized writhing dragons and a carnelian agate finial. Next to the table are Régence style chairs in the French fashion of the 18th century, but intriguingly these are reproductions made in the late-19th century and covered in panels of genuine late-17th century Brussels fabric showing birds and stylized foliage.

Under the stairs sits a Régence style giltwood sofa (French, circa 1710-1730) upholstered in early-18th century Gobelins tapestry, depicting Athena, the Greek goddess of war, fertility, arts and wisdom. On the sideboard is a reliquary of a female saint containing a fragment of bone. Although the saint remains unidentified, the staff has dubbed her Saint Cecilia, whose feast day is Doris Duke's birthday, and fittingly is a patron saint of music.

In the middle of the room is an Italian baroque walnut and gilt center table (partially 17th century with later additions) with an octagonal top on four upturned dolphin supports, that are in keeping with Rough Point's oceanside location. On the table is a large turquoise-glazed jardinière of the Ming dynasty of the 16th or 17th century, which Doris Duke liked to fill with huge arrangements of fresh flowers from the cutting garden north of the house.

The painting in the stair hall is a *Portrait of Angelo Poliziano*, oil on panel. The subject has been confirmed as a copy of a detail from a fresco by Ghirlandaio in Florence. Doris Duke, however, was certain the canvas was painted by Sandro Botticelli and went to some lengths to prove it. Regardless of its provenance, it was one of her favorite pieces. A long inscription on the back of the picture by an Italian art scholar asserts the Botticelli attribution, but several modern scholars agree that the work is not that of the master, but an effort by an accomplished anonymous artist about a generation later, approximately 1550.

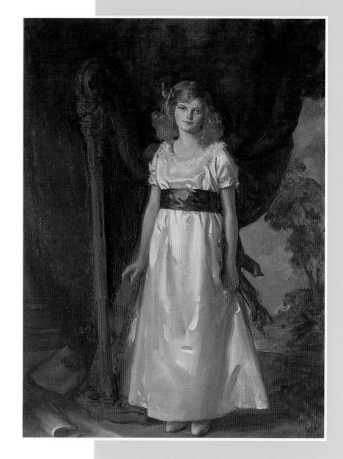

Portrait of Doris Duke, Age Twelve, *John Da Costa, United States; oil on canvas, 1924. This portrait was painted the year the Duke family moved into Rough Point. Doris Duke recalled always being impatient for the sittings to end, so that she could join her friends at Bailey's Beach.*

The Dining Room

The Dining Room at Rough Point is one of many spaces in the house that was substantially altered by the Dukes and their architect, Horace Trumbauer, in 1922. As built for Frederick Vanderbilt, the Dining Room was a large space, but there was a hallway and at least one small room to the north side. The Dukes decided to clear away the service areas and create a dining room that occupied the full width of the house. The ceiling was replaced with a deeply coffered, molded plaster, *faux* wood pattern, in keeping with the English manorial style of the house. The room was lit by two late-19th-century French chandeliers, set in such a way to suggest that the room was meant to accommodate a table seating about thirty people with style and elegance. Perhaps, for a time, it was used that way, but tradition suggests that neither Doris Duke nor her mother cared for entertaining on a large scale, and certainly now the room arrangement is remarkably intimate.

Straight ahead from the main door, one is faced with a large cast-stone fireplace surmounted by one of the greatest art works in the house, *The Annunciation*, painted by Palma il Vecchio in about 1525 and one of the earliest works that the Dukes brought here. Matching Régence style sofas covered in 17th-century fabric flank the fireplace, along with side tables, silver lamps and small *objets d'art*. The space looks like a large sitting room, but then one notices a Flemish Renaissance style table by the seaside windows. Large by most standards, the table seats fourteen but looks small in this space. Although fourteen chairs were restored for use here, six more are stowed in an attic space; household staff remember that Doris Duke seldom hosted more than six or eight guests for dinner.

The Dining Room contains three beautifully preserved tapestries, including a lavish Louis XIV period piece. This tapestry was made in the late-17th century in Beauvais, France, to praise the glory of the king in the style of the day. There are two coats of arms in the center—the royal arms and the arms of Navarre, the king's family seat—flanked by winged nymphs reclining on clouds on a background patterned with fleur-de-lis. A pair of Brussels Gothic tapestries from the early-16th century hang at either end of the dining table. Much less imaginatively woven than the French example, these tapestries crowd many human figures and many details into scenes of courtly life. As such, they are intriguing pictures of contemporary life, at least among the wealthy and powerful of Europe five hundred years ago.

Fruit Basket, *workshop of Luca della Robbia, Florence, Italy; glazed earthenware, 16th century. A pair of these whimsical baskets adorn the Dining Room and include not only fruits and vegetables, but a friendly looking frog and a small lizard.*

Fluted maiolica basin, Venice, Italy; tin-glazed earthenware, circa 1560. In the narrative style of the time, this piece was not made for practical use, but solely as a support for the illustration of the Three Graces.

One of the most wonderful art works at Rough Point is the painting, The Annunciation, *hanging over the fireplace in the Dining Room. Painted in northern Italy in about 1525 by Palma il Vecchio (Palma the Elder), it originally was installed in a church in the city of Bergamo, until baroque tastes called for newer pictures. Family inventories indicate that it was one of the first art works to be hung in the house when the Dukes moved in, and it remains there still.*

—◆—〓◆〓—◆—

Coronation Scene, *Flanders; silk and wool tapestry, early-16th century. This colorful scene in a royal court depicts the grand occasion of a coronation, possibly depicting the French king, Louis XII.*

Exemplary of the high regard in which Doris Duke held antique textiles is a Régence room divider screen near the fireplace, made in the French royal Savonnerie factory about 1720. The four panels of the screen contain woven scenes from the fables of la Fontaine. The style and the subject matter of the screen also relate to the largest furniture group in Rough Point, the Louis XVI chairs and sofa in the Music Room.

Staff at Rough Point recall visits by Imelda Marcos, the former Philipine first lady, accompanied by two or more guards. The guards did not have their own room, but sat upright in chairs all night in Mrs. Marcos's room, and there always seemed to be an air of mystery about the visits. Part of that may have been due to the fact that television trucks often sat outside the gates in anticipation of Mrs. Marcos's arrival, followed by the inevitable planning for a discrete exit when the time came. Mrs. Marcos often liked to sing in the Dining Room just before dinner, though the staff called it "singing for her supper," and privately Doris Duke was not fond of the serenades. Most dinners were quiet by comparison.

Despite the arrangement of this room for relatively intimate dining, Doris Duke seldom used it during the nights when she dined alone. Breakfast was always in her own room, as was dinner on most nights. Lunch was usually served in the Solarium. Still, the Dining Room was as carefully assembled and decorated as any room in the house and was always available for an elegant dinner, with the sea breeze blowing in the windows and dozens of candles lending a warm glow.

When Doris Duke traveled from house to house, she often took favorite things with her, including food, wine, art works, furniture, clothing and dogs, but one of the most widely traveled objects was a sterling silver swan. Tiffany & Co. made this large centerpiece in 1874 and displayed an identical one at the Centennial Exposition in 1876. Although it was available on order through the company, it appears that few were made. Miss Duke bought it at a Sotheby's auction in 1988, and thereafter carried it about on her journeys to her homes in Honolulu, Beverly Hills, Newport, New York, and Somerville, New Jersey.

The Kitchen

The kitchen at Rough Point was another area that was rebuilt in 1922, when James B. Duke bought the property and did a very thorough renovation. The white ceramic tiles were typical of the period, and because dirt could be easily identified on the gleaming white surfaces, conveyed the feeling of sanitary conditions. Several decades later, Doris Duke decided to make a few changes to the old design. An interior decorator friend persuaded her to paint the ceiling and trim dark blue, a tradition that continues today. The kitchen fireplace was constructed at about the same time. If one looks carefully above the fireplace, the arch of an old ventilator hood can be seen. In the 1920s, a large stove resided where the hearth now lies, and cooking vapors were exhausted through the hood. The grate in the wall remains over the ventilator opening.

To the left stands a polished and imposing presence, an oak and brass ice box installed during the early renovation. The interior is white ceramic, for the same reasons of cleanliness, and it also helped contain the water from the melting one-hundred-pound block of ice. By 1958, Doris Duke had a mechanical cooling system added to the icebox, although the pump and electric motor are in the basement, so as not to intrude on the tranquility of the kitchen. Another early appliance is the low, foursquare humidor directly adjacent to the door on the right side. Mr. Duke loved cigars and apparently kept an ample supply at hand under the best conditions in this humidor, fittingly covered in white ceramic tile. The kitchen is not extravagant, because the Dukes were not fond of large dinner parties, but it is certainly set up to handle daily dining and frequent small dinner groups. The full set of copper cookware hanging from the pot rack was a favorite of the cooks, and the maids were kept busy polishing, due to the effects of cooking on the stove and the salt air of the seashore. The entire kitchen was cleaned daily top to bottom.

The Butler's Pantry is just to the east of the kitchen, and there is a pass-through for food to be placed on trays or kept in the big warming oven on the right side. The pantry is furnished with a large icebox, identical to the one in the kitchen, and also equipped with mechanical cooling that operates from the basement below. A large sink with varnished ash drainboards is thoughtfully placed where the dishwasher could gaze out at the ocean while elbow deep in

Even at a place like Rough Point, modern technology was adopted when its presence would serve a purpose. One such example was the purchase of a fax machine for the house, at a time when faxes were an unusual and special means of communication. Similar machines were installed in all of Miss Duke's houses, and daily business was communicated and transacted between them and Duke Farms in New Jersey. One of the most important uses of the fax was to transmit recipes from one house to the others (Shangri La, in Hawaii; Duke Farms; the New York apartment; and Falcon's Lair in Beverly Hills), so that new dishes she liked would be part of the recipe library in every kitchen.

sudsy water. In the surrounding drawers and cupboards are the sets of dishes, breakfast sets, napkins and placemats, trays, decanters and serving pieces that even a house with modest entertaining needs would require. Out of sight to the left is the silver room, housing a silver service for forty, tea, chocolate and coffee sets, chafing dishes, serving dishes and platters, salts and pepper dispensers, and silver plates, bowls, tankards, candlesticks, and special utensils. Everything is an eclectic mix of antique pieces and 20th-century items, purchased either by Doris Duke or her parents. Household staffers have indicated that Doris Duke liked having the antiques and enjoyed collecting them upon occasion, but she did not often use the oldest or most ornate pieces. Here, as throughout the main house, everything remains as it was the last time Doris Duke was in residence.

It may be a unique feature of Rough Point, among all the large Bellevue Avenue houses, that many staff areas had views equal to the best in the house. Most utility areas were in the basement, and when they were above ground level, the view was often to a driveway or back yard. While even at Rough Point the staff living and work areas lack the drama of the formal rooms, no one can deny the beautiful marine vistas available through any window. The Staff Dining Room is a light and airy space, cozy with a large fireplace and bookshelves, where the house staff could relax with a pleasant meal when activities in the house were not too hectic. And, since Miss Duke was often in residence no more than a third of the year, one can imagine that staff life here could be quite pleasant. In general, there were two house staff on duty throughout the year, and in the off seasons their duties were to circulate through the house, cleaning all the rooms, always ready for "The Boss" to return.

There are dozens of cookbooks at Rough Point and a series of loose-leaf binders with her favorite recipes in them. Some are typed, a few handwritten, and some photocopied from The New York Times *and other sources. But as much as Doris Duke liked her standard recipes, sometimes she liked to be surprised. She once asked her cook for something new, and the special dish was a chicken soup, "Julia Child's Tureen Supreme." It became a favorite, to the extent that the cook became weary of making it. Other beloved recipes included bouillabaisse "She loved my bouillabaisse," noted the cook. "And she likes pot-au-feu, which is a French stew – ah, she loves that French stew… In the summer she likes curried chicken with bananas. She loves that dish. And then she likes a lot of soufflés, of course."*

The Pine Room

The second floor of Rough Point was Doris Duke's private retreat within a house that was itself intensely private. The part of this floor that is open to the public presents the most important rooms and gives a clear picture of Doris Duke's preferences for decoration and furnishing in her private spaces. Her preference was always for intimate spaces, often a challenge in a building with the vast open space of Rough Point, but the second floor lent itself to this desire more easily than the first. The large landing immediately conveys the effect of lower ceilings—ten feet, compared to twelve to twenty-six feet on the first floor. Although her exquisite collection of antique oriental carpets could not be left on the polished oak floors, a huge, 17th-century, English table stands opposite her bedroom door, adorned with a selection of her favorite Chinese porcelains. Once again her taste in oriental art is present in the form of a jardinière and a pair of large punchbowls and the large famille verte jars that are especially graceful and rare survivals.

Remaining on the table are five stacks of magazines and catalogs that she read and referred to regularly. House staff say that she would keep materials on the table as long as she was interested in them and then discard them as she pleased. Catalogs from the major auction houses of the world that were kept here often included items that she bought for collections at Rough Point, or for the American furniture collection at Samuel Whitehorne House— also in Newport—for her houses in New Jersey, New York, Beverly Hills or Honolulu. Her favorite magazines included: *Vogue, Apollo, House and Garden, Connoisseur, Antiques* and *Architectural Digest*. Although she was not a constant reader of books, Doris Duke read three daily papers, *The New York Times, The Wall Street Journal* and *The Washington Post*.

The decoration of the hall itself is simple and elegant in an informal way that contrasts with the imposing first floor rooms. The white-painted walls and trim help to keep a feeling of light in an area with few windows, all north facing. Below the chair rail is a simple, cheerful strip of green trellis wallpaper, printed on a white background. This paper makes a telling connection with one of Doris Duke's best friends, Alletta Morris (later Alletta Morris McBean), whom she knew from childhood in Newport. Chepstow, the McBean house just down the street from Rough Point, has the same wallpaper design in several areas. The carpet made to match the wallpaper colors is a reproduction to replicate the threadbare original. The art works on the second floor are mostly prints and drawings, generally depicting flowers or mythological and classical scenes.

Furniture in the hall is really incidental to its use, and so everything here is decorative, rather than serving a practical purpose. However, as decorative pieces, they are well chosen. Two George III satinwood and marquetry tables, walnut wall brackets, and carved and gilt mirrors share the hallway with upholstered benches and chairs of similar styles.

The Pine Room adjoins the hallway and offers yet another contrasting and unique decorative style. Twenty-seven imported Régence panels in a clear natural finish line the room, along with carvings and moldings, giving the room a very warm, cozy feeling. While the Pine Room looks like a pleasant study or sitting room, it was used almost exclusively as Doris Duke's music room on the second floor. Although the concert grand piano in the formal Music Room was the better instrument, she preferred to play and practice in the Pine Room, using a Knabe baby grand piano on a daily basis. The big Sony reel-to-reel tape recorder stands nearby, just as it did when she recorded her own compositions and arrangements, to listen to them and make further refinements. To date, the tapes themselves have not been found.

Doris Duke's passion in instrumental music was jazz, which she loved to play herself, although she also invited jazz musicians to Rough Point occasionally. Pianist Joe Castro was a good friend for many years, and for a brief time Miss Duke had her own recording company, Clover Records, primarily to publish Castro's music. She also loved to sing, at one time joining a Baptist church choir in New Jersey. The choir director said that she had a soft voice, not really suited to solos, but she did well with the group. She practiced her singing regularly with a voice coach from Brooklyn, who traveled to either Duke Farms or Rough Point to instruct her student.

The Incas, *Joseph Dufour and Compagnie (1797-1835), Paris, France; ink on paper, circa 1820. The faltering Dufour wallpaper company began producing panoramic papers in the early-19th century, and had great success with a variety of scenes. Some, like* The Incas, *were based largely on artists' conceptions but were still considered educational and entertaining.*

Miss Duke's Room

Doris Duke's bedroom was more than a sleeping chamber. She began her day with breakfast in bed, often greeting all of her dogs before she arose for the day. Even a very large malamute, Kimo, came in and often climbed on the bed after breakfast, upsetting the dishes and causing chaos. She had the greatest forbearance toward her dogs, and their affection for her was unquestioned. Activities during the day often included a swim in the ocean from Midship Rock, just to the right of the ocean view from the bedroom window. Without steps, ladders, or a smooth beach, Doris Duke swam daily by climbing down the rocks into the water and back out again. Although a groundskeeper was always on duty at the gate in the fence nearby, she never requested help getting in or out of the water, even in her seventies.

Looking upwards from the stair landing on the second floor, a pair of tall candelabra flanking the double doors to the master bedroom herald the special sanctuary created within. Even in a house filled with Louis XVI period furniture, the candelabra stand out; they are covered in mother-of-pearl, and the trim, ten candle arms and figure of Victory on top are of gilt bronze. Made in Paris about 1810, these give the visitor a hint of Doris Duke's motif for decorating her own bedroom.

Stepping into the room, one is struck by the elegant contrast of the black carpet with the yellow walls and the purple furniture and curtain fabrics. One can only imagine the impact of the room prior to 1980, when the walls and carpet were also purple. The curtains and a daybed are both covered in tones of purple, and there is furniture upholstered in purple more brilliant yet. Six side chairs and a settee are covered in bright purple and metallic gold fabric, and all of their frame surfaces are faced with mother-of-pearl. This rare suite of furniture, of Charles X style and probably made in France about 1820, also includes two console tables, two wall mirrors, a center table and a writing table, all covered in glimmering mother-of-pearl. The smaller tables hold various mother-of-pearl garnitures, lovingly collected by their owner during her world travels over the years: a clock, candlesticks, a desk set and small boxes. A tall and imposing secretary desk of

Up to about 1975, her bedroom was decorated almost entirely in purple. The annunciators for the staff bells still list it as the "Mauve Room." At about that time, though, she decided to redecorate and had the Newport Restoration Foundation paint crew come in and paint the mauve walls yellow, as they are today, and the carpet was dyed black. A tall, fall-front secretary anchors a corner of the room, aglow with mother-of-pearl on the outer surfaces, and inlaid with ivory, tortoiseshell and exotic woods throughout the interior. The small Renoir that hangs in front of a large mirror over the fireplace has been in the same location since its purchase in 1959. It is the only painting in the room.

In a large and richly furnished house such as Rough Point, a room that takes the visitor by surprise must be either particularly lavish, or unique in some way. Certainly, the master bedroom, with its twelve-piece suite of mother-of-pearl covered furniture, is almost dreamlike in its rarity. The French 18th-century suite of sofa, tables and chairs is augmented by a large secretary-bookcase made in Portuguese Goa in the same period and many small pieces, from dishes to candlesticks. The subdued shimmer of the mother-of-pearl, contrasted by purple and gold upholstery and the black carpet, conveys a stunning example of Doris Duke's taste for her personal chamber.

separate manufacture stands next to the bed, its surfaces covered in a mixture of mother-of-pearl, ivory, tortoiseshell and exotic woods. It was probably made about 1800 in Goa, a Portuguese colony in western India.

If the mother-of-pearl pieces are overwhelming at first, there are many small, personal touches in the bedroom that hint at the personality of Doris Duke. On the secretary are a group of three small, silver loving cups—trophies of her childhood days at Bailey's Beach, just down the road. Dancing the tango, playing tennis and constructing sand sculptures are among the subjects of a total of twelve little trophies in the collection. Some of these activities she shared with her good friend Alletta Morris, who helped found the Preservation Society of Newport County. On the lacquered breakfast table is an array of small collectibles, such as any traveler might collect, and yet this wealthy collector of the finest antiques had them spread out on a table in her room: a fish carved from a seashell, ceramic and glass dishes and snuff boxes of silver and porcelain. They are touching souvenirs from a life spent in homes across the world.

The finishing touch for this very personal room is a small painting by Pierre-August Renoir, *Fille Cousant* (Young Girl Sewing), painted by the Impressionist master in 1875. This is one of the few late-19th-century paintings Doris Duke owned, and she purchased it in 1959, when she was looking for some of the major decorative pieces for the house. It is a wonderful example of the artist's light palette and delicate brushwork of that period, painted just four years after Renoir gained public recognition at the official art Salon in Paris.

Adjoining the master bedroom is a dressing room equipped with some splendid furnishings. There is a whimsical French chandelier, with scrolling bronze arms and tendrils, bedecked with green glass leaves and colorful porcelain flowers. The sink and bathtub have faucets and spouts in the form of dolphins. Although this tub does not offer hot and cold running salt water, a large antique tub in the adjoining Blue Room does. Doris Duke firmly believed in the beneficial effects of seawater, so her indoor pool and one special tub offered salt-water bathing, in ocean water, free of any chemical treatment.

Over the bathtub is an antique French barometer, decorated with a wonderful reverse-painted and gilt dial. Although it was no longer functional, some of the house staff set the barometer's indicator to match Miss Duke's mood on any given day, from "Tempête," or tempestuous, to "Beau Temps," or good weather. She never seemed to notice this signal of her demeanor.

Even this small room has its share of exceptional furniture. There are two Empire cut glass pieces, made in France about 1810. A small pedestal base table serves as a lamp stand, while a sparkling dressing table shows off thirteen gold pieces of a particularly elegant dresser set from Tiffany and Company. The dressing table strongly resembles an even more opulent piece in the Louvre, and is thought to have been designed by the French master, Georges Jacob.

The Solarium

The Solarium may be the most striking room in Rough Point, which is a strong statement for such a grand house. First one passes from the subdued lighting of the surrounding rooms into the sunlit intensity of the outdoors and is immediately taken by the dramatic sweep of the coastline, combining land, sea, and sky into a landscape painting that is both architectural and natural. It is a room that was cherished by its owners. In effect, it is a focal point for the surrounding seascape and for dramatic shifts in the weather. One of the greatest treats for a visitor to Rough Point is to witness a towering summer thunderstorm sweep in across the sea and darken the sky. One has the feeling of being right in the seascape, while remaining safe within a beautiful porch.

In function, the Solarium is a comfortable sitting room—where, in fact, Doris Duke often took lunch, made phone calls, met with the board of the Newport Restoration Foundation and conducted other business. To the east of the Solarium the view is of Easton Bay and Ochre Point, where the seaside homes in the Bellevue Avenue area are lined up along the Cliff Walk. In the distance are Sachuest Point, Second Beach, and Little Compton. With reasonable visibility Cuttyhunk can be seen a little further out to sea, and on a truly clear day there appears a vague line floating above the horizon that is Martha's Vineyard. The straight-ahead view is a rocky ravine descending to the ocean under a wooden bridge on the Cliff Walk, and a wide, usually empty, horizon on the Atlantic Ocean. Toward the west is the promontory of Midship Rock, where Doris Duke swam in the ocean. Although there is no beach and no steps, even into her seventies she dove into the water and found a way back out again, despite the ocean waves and barnacle-covered rocks.

The furnishings in the Solarium are fitting for an informal room in a formal house. Two overstuffed chairs and a sofa covered in brown velvet comprise virtually the only group of modern furniture in the house. The carpet is a replica; the original antique oriental carpet was removed to accommodate tours. Two Roman style bronze busts sit atop purple-streaked gray and white marble columns flanking the southern view. The ceiling is painted with a sky-blue background and clouds, and a pergola around the sides gives the impression that one is standing in an open-air courtyard. Rows of plants and some climbing vines help to complete the feeling of a space that could easily be outdoors.

The best tales about the Solarium involve Doris Duke's animals, and not just the Malamute who sidled up to Jacqueline Onassis's plate and ate her lunch at one gulp. Rough Point was famous for its camels for a few years. Doris Duke bought a Boeing 737 plane, and the deal included a pair of camels from the Middle Eastern owners. The two Bactrian camels, Princess and Baby, lived at Rough Point each summer. They were sheltered under a large tent next to the Solarium. Guests could feed them graham crackers through a "camel gate" in the French doors. Hikers on the Cliff Walk reported seeing giraffes, llamas and other exotic creatures, though it was only the camels of Rough Point.

The Solarium, a 1922 addition to Rough Point, was designed by architect Horace Trumbauer to resemble an outdoor space. Rusticated walls resemble limestone, and there is a pergola around the sides for hanging plants and a sky scene painted on the ceiling to emphasize the outdoor feeling.

Doris Duke was renowned for her love of animals, and she always had eight to twelve dogs at Rough Point, many of which relaxed in the solarium with their mistress. A Sharpei named Chairman Mao survives, and a greyhound and a large husky have come to the museum from the local animal shelter to continue the tradition. The camels, her most exotic animals, no longer summer here.

Doris Duke and the NRF

In 1968 Doris Duke began her first serious efforts in historic preservation with the founding of the Newport Restoration Foundation. Her love of good craftsmanship and aesthetic detail found expression here in her genuine concern for the rapidly disappearing architecture of 18th-century Newport.

In the 1960s Newport had, within its borders, one of the largest collections of 18th-century architecture anywhere in the country, but this wonderful historical asset went largely unrecognized as it had for decades. Newporters had always made do with old structures rather than building new, and most of the city's colonial houses had slowly deteriorated into tenements and cold-water flats for navy and industrial housing. By the mid-20th century, the local architectural heritage was tattered. During this time, residence after residence was routinely demolished, often in the destructive guise of urban renewal. These losses started to reverse in the mid-sixties when a very successful grassroots organization called Operation Clapboard rescued almost sixty early houses in Newport by finding interested private preservationists who would purchase important houses and restore them appropriately. There was, however, a limit to what most private efforts could achieve given the sheer size of the task.

The possibilities for more extensive preservation efforts came to the notice of Doris Duke, and in 1968 the Newport Restoration Foundation (NRF) picked up where Operation Clapboard's efforts left off. With her enormous resources, Doris Duke undertook the preservation of many of the most deteriorated structures from the 18th and early-19th centuries. At the height of its efforts, the Foundation employed over seventy architects, painters, carpenters, and other skilled artisans. Many of the houses on which they worked had to be moved quickly to escape the wrecking ball. Although most of the structures were from Newport there are a few that came from out of town and three that were from out of Rhode Island altogether.

Most NRF projects were the structures in the worst condition and unlikely to be saved by anyone who was not prepared to invest considerably more capital than the completed house was worth. For example, it was not unusual for the Foundation to purchase a house for $10,000 and

Pictured at left is the Langley House, circa 1807, located at 28 Church Street and on the right is the Dr. Cotton House, circa 1720, at 32 Church Street. These are but two of more than eighty buildings the NRF restored in the process of preserving Newport's 18th-century buildings and streetscape.

Samuel Whitehorne House was one of the last buildings restored by Newport Restoration Foundation. It opened to the public in 1975 as a museum of Newport furniture, and it contains the largest collection of locally created masterpieces in the city.

invest an additional $80,000-$100,000 when the market value after restoration was only $50,000.

By the time the Foundation stopped actively restoring houses in 1985, eighty-four properties, or roughly one-quarter of Newport's 18th-century housing stock had been lovingly restored by NRF craftsmen. The NRF continues to own, maintain, and preserve the houses that were originally restored by Doris Duke's generosity.

Although preservation was only a passing interest before she founded the NRF, afterward it was a passion. She was personally vested in the preservation of each house and often offered her opinion on interior and exterior colors from the historically researched color charts. Through the remainder of her life, she donated more to historic preservation than to any other of her many philanthropic pursuits.

In addition to buildings, Doris Duke also started collecting 18th-century furniture for the NRF. Her eye and that of her agents was excellent, and she assembled an outstanding collection of mid-18th-century Newport furniture, which today still is one of the only places in which Newport furniture can be seen in its native environment. This fine collection of American decorative arts was placed in the Samuel Whitehorne House, an important Federal-period building on Thames Street, that was subsequently opened to the public as a museum and remains another popular public site of the Restoration Foundation and a center for scholarly study of Newport furniture.

Today the NRF is a vital and lively organization, which holds one of the largest collections of early vernacular American architecture anywhere in the country, as well as collections of American and European fine and decorative arts. It is a preservation and museum organization whose creation and continuing vitality are the remarkable legacy of Doris Duke. She was someone who saw the depth and breadth of Newport's history and, through her vision and extraordinary generosity, chose to offer the city's past to future generations.